NINJA KID 7

NINJA TOYS!

Scholastic Press
An imprint of Scholastic Australia Pty Limited (ABN 11 000 614 577)
PO Box 579 Gosford NSW 2250
www.scholastic.com.au

Part of the Scholastic Group
Sydney • Auckland • New York • Toronto • London • Mexico City
• New Delhi • Hong Kong • Buenos Aires • Puerto Rico

First published by Scholastic Australia in 2021.

ISBN 978-93-5471-988-2

A catalogue record for this book is available from the National Library of Australia

Typeset in Bizzle-Chizzle, featuring Hola Bisou and Handblock.

This reprint edition : April 2026

Printed in India at MicroPrints India, New Delhi

ANH DO

illustrated by Anton Emdin

NINJA KID 7

NINJA TOYS!

A Scholastic Press book
from Scholastic Australia

ONE

My name is **Nelson Kane**. I used to be an average, everyday kid. In fact, I was a bit of a NERD!

But when I woke up on my tenth birthday, I had become . . .

NiNJA KiD!

I inherited my ninja powers from my dad, who mysteriously disappeared when I was little.

For a long time, I had no idea what happened to him. But now I know . . .

DR KANE put a microchip into my dad's neck, which has **brainwashed** him! Now my dad is the **ULTIMATE NINJA**.

The **ULTIMATE NINJA** is helping Dr Kane wreak havoc on Duck Creek, the town where I live, along with Dr Kane's smartypants chipmunk, **EINSTEIN**.

My dream is to rescue my dad from Dr Kane and bring him back home.

I live in a house on a **junkyard** with my **mum**, **Grandma** and my **cousin Kenny**, who is always **hungry!** Kenny would eat the leg off a chair if you put some sauce on it!

But luckily he doesn't have to, because Mum is a really good cook.

Living in **Duck Creek** is **awesome**, it's such a cool little town. But it's constantly under **threat** from **DR KANE**.

CRaZY RoBoTS!
HuGe DiNoSauRS!

There are three reasons Dr Kane wants everyone to leave Duck Creek:

1. He's **jealous** he didn't get ninja powers like me and my dad.
2. He wants to dig up Duck Creek to find the rare **hypno diamonds**.
3. He is pure **EVIL!**

Whenever Dr Kane attacks Duck Creek, I turn into **NiNJA KiD** and Kenny turns into my trusty **sidekick**, **H-DUDE**.

But H-Dude and Ninja Kid don't work alone. Our best friends, Sarah and Tiffany, are always on hand to help us out. They're **athletic**, they're **smart**, and I'm really glad they're on our side!

And we get tons of help from Grandma and her AMAZING `inventions`. Even though they don't always do what they're supposed to . . .

Like her `Never-Get-Lost Umbrella`, which will come and find you if you leave it somewhere. Except it always turns up at the wrong time!

Or the **Robotic Pot-Plant Holder** that's supposed to move a plant to wherever the sun is shining . . .

. . . but it's more interested in chasing me and Kenny around the house!

Through all our battles with Dr Kane, Kenny and I have managed to keep our superhero identities a secret.

Not even Sarah and Tiffany know that we are **NiNJA KiD** and **H-DUDE**.

Now, Kenny and I have a new secret . . . what we bought Sarah for her birthday!

TWO

Sarah promised us her birthday party was going to be a little different. And she wasn't wrong!

Sarah and her mum had transformed the back of her house into a **ROCK-CLIMBING** wall!

Of course, Charles Brock started with the most difficult climb. Charles is the son of the Mayor. He's also the school bully. He's meaner than a Viking whose pants are too tight!

Charles is always trying to make himself feel **better** by making everyone else feel **worse**.

When Charles reached the top of the wall, he **banged his chest** to show off.

I desperately wanted to use my **NINJA SKILLS** to prove I was a better climber than Charles. But I couldn't risk giving away my secret identity. So I had to climb r e a l l y s l o w l y. I must have looked like a monkey who had just woken up!

Sarah is really fit and completed the hardest climb easily. So did Tiffany. They didn't show off like Charles.

But not everyone was nailing the climbing wall. Kenny made climbing a lot harder by bringing snacks up the wall with him!

After the climbing, we went inside so Sarah could open her presents. I had spent **aaaages** thinking about what to buy Sarah for her birthday. I wanted her to really like it!

And I didn't have to wait long to find out what she thought . . . because she opened my present **first!**

'I saw you reading the book,' I said. 'Looked like you were enjoying it!'

'It's my favourite book ever!' Sarah replied. 'Thank you so much for this!'

Sarah opened Kenny's present next. It was a figurine of Wolf Girl's best friend, Sunrise The Wolf.

'I love Sunrise!' Sarah said.

Tiffany gave Sarah a funny **T-shirt!**

Charles gave Sarah the **biggest** figurine of the Golden Unicorn I'd ever seen. It was huge! When you pressed her back, she took three steps and did a spin kick.

'Sarah definitely likes my present the best!' Charles gloated to me and Kenny. 'Maybe you should think a little **bigger** next time, losers!'

Even though I was used to Charles bragging all the time, I couldn't help feeling a little **deflated**. I was like a balloon at the end of a party.

Sarah seemed to really love the giant Golden Unicorn figurine Charles had given her.

As we walked back outside to play party games, Sarah turned to me and Kenny. 'Your presents were so thoughtful, guys. But I wouldn't care if you bought me a couple of old tomatoes. I'm just happy to spend time with two of my favourite people.'

I was so chuffed I turned the colour of a tomato!

'Well, at least we know what to get her next year,' whispered Kenny. 'A bag of tomatoes!'

Next, we played heaps of fun party games, but the crowd favourite was the **donuts on a string** race.

Kenny was really, really good at that game!

But Charles won. By cheating . . . as usual!

After the games, everyone sang **Happy Birthday** to Sarah and ate a slice of Wolf Girl birthday **cake**, which Sarah and her mum made. It was **wolf-a-licious!**

We were **hot** and **sweaty** after all the birthday games, so Sarah cooled everyone down with something she had made for the **Science Fair** . . . a fan powered by a lemon battery.

‘That lemon fan is **OK**,’ Charles said. ‘But **I’m** definitely going to **WIN** the Science Fair tomorrow.’

‘**Mo**dest as ever, Charles!’ Tiffany said.

‘**It**’s not just *my* opinion,’ Charles replied. ‘**My** dad said my project is better than anything **Albert Einstein** invented at my age.’

'What's your Science Fair project, Nelson?' Sarah asked.

'It's a secret,' I replied.

'But let's just say it's going to cause an **eruption!**' Kenny cried out.

'Kenny!' I exclaimed. 'You are **hopeless** at secrets!'

Kenny could not keep anything to himself. If there was a movie called **Blabbermouth**, he would be the star for sure!

THREE

Next morning, Kenny and I practised our Science Fair presentations. Kenny made edible crystal candy sticks in different colours and flavours for his project. It had taken all his willpower not to eat them before the Science Fair started.

It took me ages, but I managed to create an **exploding volcano!** I made the volcano out of papier-mâché. Then, to make it erupt, I filled it with orange soft drink and dropped lollies into it!

'Very impressive, boys!' Mum said.

'We learnt from the master!' I said, pointing to Grandma.

'Funny you should say that,' Grandma said, 'because you're not the only ones with **new inventions**.'

She threw an old gardening glove onto the kitchen table.

'Sorry to say it, Grandma,' Kenny said, 'but gardening gloves have already been invented.'

'This is no **ordinary** glove,' Grandma replied, pulling her new invention onto her right hand.

'I think this might actually be my **GREATEST invention ever!**' Grandma said. 'It's definitely my favourite.'

Now Kenny and I were super excited to see what this special glove could do.

'I call it the **Glove of Life**,' Grandma said. 'Watch closely!'

She pointed the glove at a little toy fish sitting in a bowl of water. Grandma pressed a button on the knuckle of the gardening glove . . .

Nothing happened.

Grandma pressed the button again . . .

Still nothing.

Grandma pressed the button a **third** time and . . .

The toy fish turned into a **REAL** goldfish and started swimming around the bowl!

'WHOA!' I said. 'You can make toys **come to life!'**

'Your grandma is a genius,' said Mum.

'A **total** genius,' Kenny said.

'Will that fish stay alive forever now?' I asked.

'Or until I do this–' Grandma pressed the button twice.

Nothing happened.

'As you can see, it's still got a few kinks!' Grandma said. 'Sometimes I can't get it to work at all.'

She pushed the button twice again . . .

The fish changed back to a wind-up toy!

'I don't care about the kinks, Grandma,' I said. 'This is definitely your **coolest** invention ever!'

'I agree with Nelson!' Kenny said.

'I agree with Kenny!' Mum said.

'Can I try it?' Kenny asked. 'I want to bring Speedy to life!'

'You can both try it out when we have more time,' Grandma said. 'Right now, I have another invention that needs my attention. And you boys need to take your **own inventions** to the Science Fair!'

'I have to hurry to a cleaning job,' Mum said. 'Do us proud, you two!'

'Let's go, Kenny,' I said. 'I need time to set up.'

I raced to the cupboard to grab the bag of lollies I needed for my volcano.

They were gone!

I hurried to the fridge to grab the bottle of orange soft drink . . .

It was empty!

'Who ate all my lollies and drank all my soft drink?!' I asked, full of panic.

'Umm . . . Grandma loves soft drink,' Kenny said. 'And your mum loves lollies . . . so I'd say that's where they went.'

When I stared at Kenny, he confessed.

'I'm sorry, Nelson! I was trying so hard not to eat **my** experiment that I ate **yours** instead!'

'What about the soft drink?' I asked.

'Lollies and orange soft drink are the **perfect combo!**' said Kenny.

'My project is **useless** without lollies and soft drink,' I said. 'I'm going to **fail** the Science Fair!'

'Unless you bring a **different** project,' Kenny said.

'How am I going to come up with a new Science Fair project in a couple of minutes?!' I asked.

'You don't have to,' Kenny said. 'Grandma came up with one for you!'

'I can't take the **Glove of Life!**' I said. 'It's Grandma's favourite invention.'

'It's also her **best** invention!' Kenny said. 'We need to show the world!'

'It's up to Grandma to show the world,' I said. 'She wouldn't want us demonstrating its powers without her permission.'

'Whenever Grandma **doesn't** want us to touch something,' Kenny said, 'she makes a big point of telling us. But she didn't say anything about the glove.'

'It still doesn't feel right,' I said.

'You know what doesn't feel right?' Kenny said. 'Letting Charles be the **king** of the Science Fair when he doesn't deserve it!'

I stared at the glove, torn by indecision.

'Whatever you decide,' Kenny said, 'decide **quickly!** We're running super late!'

Kenny hurried towards the door with his crystal candy sticks. I didn't have another second to think about it. I put the **Glove of Life**, the wind-up fish and the fishbowl into my schoolbag and raced out the door.

FOUR

We arrived just in time for the Science Fair. Mr Fletcher had decorated our classroom. It looked awesome!

Mr Fletcher even dressed up as a **Wacky Scientist** in preparation for his role as Chief Judge!

But Mr Fletcher wasn't the only one judging the Science Fair. This year, the fair had a sponsor, **Gorilla Gadgets**, and their mascot, Gary the Gorilla, was also there to judge the projects.

'If Gary really likes an invention,' Mr Fletcher told the class, 'it could become part of Gorilla Gadgets' range of amazing products!'

Even though none of us had heard of **Gorilla Gadgets**, we all went completely nuts!

There were so many incredible Science Fair projects. Tiffany made a pencil rise up into the air using magnets!

Billy Bob devised an ice-cream maker which made ten different ice-cream flavours . . . **at once!**

And not just your standard flavours like chocolate, vanilla and strawberry. There was **hotdog** flavour and **spaghetti** flavour!

Mr Fletcher was impressed by Charles's project . . . a solar-powered oven **inside** a pizza box!

Kenny had shown incredible self-control to not eat his candy crystals before the Science Fair. (Even though he ate mine instead!)

Mr Fletcher and Gary the Gorilla judged my science project last. They looked **totally unimpressed** as they studied the gardening glove and the toy fish in the bowl of water.

'What's it called?' Mr Fletcher asked.

'The **Glove Of Life**,' I replied.

'Let's hope it's more interesting than it looks,' Mr Fletcher said.

I pulled Grandma's glove onto my right hand.

'Whoa, check it out!' Charles scoffed. 'Nelson's **amazing** Science Fair project is a gardening glove. Maybe he's going to plant a few seeds!'

Charles's buddies giggled like toddlers.

'It's a little more exciting than that,' I said. 'Watch and weep.'

'Oh, I'm weeping!' Charles said. 'Weeping at how **pathetic** you are!'

I pointed the glove at the wind-up toy fish, desperately hoping I could mimic Grandma and bring it to life. I took a deep breath and pressed the button on the index finger . . .

CLICK!

Nothing happened.

'I knew it!' Charles cackled. 'I know why you've got a gardening glove . . . because your science project is a **pile of manure!**'

I pressed the button again . . . still nothing.

'Alright, Nelson, now you're just wasting everyone's time,' Mr Fletcher said.

I pushed the button again and again. Still nothing happened.

Charles and his friends were laughing so loud now it was almost deafening. Some kids walked away to look at the other experiments.

'I think we've seen enough!' Gary the Gorilla said.

I was about to **give up** until Kenny piped up. 'Come on, Nelson. You can do this!'

'OK. One more try,' I replied.

I pushed the button on the glove one final time . . .

It worked!

The toy fish turned into a REAL goldfish and started swimming around the fishbowl.

The kids were blown away. So was Mr Fletcher! **'WOOOOWWWW!'** he said in a high-pitched voice.

'How does it work?' Gary the Gorilla asked, closely examining the glove on my hand.

I hadn't thought about what to say if people asked about Grandma's miraculous invention.

I needed to come up with a scientific explanation . . . and **quickly!**

'It's, it's . . .' I stammered. 'It's all an illusion!'

I quickly aimed the glove at the fish . . .

ZAP!

Luckily, the fish turned back into a toy.

'Yes, it's all a **wonderful illusion!**' Kenny added, doing his best impression of a magician's assistant!

'I don't know how you did it, Nelson,' Mr Fletcher said. 'But you've got my vote for **first prize!**'

'Mine too!' said Gary the Gorilla.

'Then it's unanimous,' Mr Fletcher said. 'Nelson is this year's Science Fair **WINNER!**'

Everyone cheered . . . except Charles.

'My experiment was real, not some stupid illusion,' he said. 'I should get first prize.'

'THE JUDGES' DECISION IS FINAL!' Gary the Gorilla yelled.

I felt guilty. **Really** guilty. Everyone had put so much thought and effort into their Science Fair projects. But I had absolutely nothing to do with the **Glove of Life**. It was all **Grandma's** incredible work.

I was super relieved when the bell rang for recess. Finally, I could forget all about Grandma's glove.

I put it in my pocket, but before I could leave the classroom, Gary the Gorilla pulled me aside.

'Congratulations, Nelson. I've decided to take the **Glove of Life** back to Gorilla Gadgets. I think it has a huge future.'

He held out his hand, waiting for me to give him the glove.

I couldn't give **Gary** the glove! It was Grandma's favourite ever invention.

'I can't give you the glove,' I said.

'Why not, Nelson?' Mr Fletcher asked. 'This is a fantastic opportunity. **Gorilla Gadgets** could help you make a lot of money.'

'Yeah, sorry,' I said. 'I've . . . um, got some **gardening** to do, so I'm going to need this. Thanks anyway!'

I **rushed out** of the classroom before Gary or Mr Fletcher could say another word.

FiVE

When I arrived in the schoolyard, someone grabbed me by the hand . . . it was Sarah! She led me away from the others.

'Where are we going?' I asked.

'I need to ask you something,' Sarah replied. 'In private.'

What could Sarah possibly want to ask me? I thought.

I came up with three possibilities:

But all my guesses were wrong!

'Nelson,' Sarah said, as we walked behind the school gym. 'Can we try the **Glove of Life** on my Wolf Girl and Sunrise figurines?'

'Sarah, I wish I could bring Wolf Girl and Sunrise to life but, like I said, it was all an **illusion.**'

'Well, can we try, Nelson? I promise I won't tell anyone.'

I knew bringing the **Glove of Life** to school was a bad idea. I also knew that using it to impress Sarah was a **bad idea** . . . but I couldn't resist!

'OK,' I said. 'But if it works, I have to turn them straight back into toys. I can't risk anyone knowing how **powerful** this invention really is.'

'Fist-bump deal!' Sarah replied, holding out her fist.

I put on Grandma's glove and aimed it at Wolf Girl and Sunrise.

ZAP!
ZAP!

It worked, first time!

Wolf Girl and Sunrise grew to full size!

Wolf Girl blinked her big brown eyes and Sunrise The Wolf stretched her long, golden body.

'Woooooowwww!' Sarah whispered.

I was **shocked**, too. It was one thing to see a wind-up fish come to life. Seeing Wolf Girl and Sunrise alive and staring back at us was **unbelievable**.

'Wolf Girl! Sunrise!' Sarah said. 'Is that really you?'

'It really is!' Wolf Girl replied.

Sunrise let out a soft, friendly howl.

'I'm Sarah, and this is Nelson,' Sarah stammered. She was **totally gobsmacked** by what was in front of her.

And I was so amazed, all I could do was wave.

'How can we help you?' Wolf Girl asked.

'You can start by telling us how any of this is possible,' Sarah said. 'You're supposed to be toys!'

'I thought so, too,' Wolf Girl said. 'But it seems that strange glove can make us real.'

Grandma's glove was proving to be more powerful than I could have imagined. I felt like I was getting in **WAAAAYYY** too deep.

We heard footsteps behind us. I turned around, but nobody was there.

'Sorry, Wolf Girl and Sunrise but I have to turn you back into toys before I get into **HUUUUUUGE trouble!**'

'Sunrise and I definitely don't want that!' Wolf Girl said. 'If you ever need us, you know what to do!'

'Bye,' I said, still looking at Wolf Girl and Sunrise in total disbelief.

'Hopefully we'll see you again!' Sarah said.

She was so excited by her favourite book characters coming to life.

'I hope so, too,' Wolf Girl replied.

Sunrise howled softly.

I aimed the glove at Wolf Girl and Sunrise and pressed the button on the Glove of Life twice . . .

CLICK! CLICK!

Nothing happened.

'Sorry,' I said. 'It's still a work in progress!'

'No need to apologise!' Wolf Girl replied.

It took **four** attempts but finally . . .

And just like that, Wolf Girl and Sunrise were toys once more.

Sarah looked **sooooooo shocked**.

'Are you OK?' I asked.

Sarah nodded. 'Thank you, Nelson, that was **amazing**.'

'I was a bit surprised myself, to be honest,' I replied.

Then we heard more footsteps. We turned to see Gary the Gorilla disappearing around the corner of the gym.

'Do you think he saw anything?' I whispered to Sarah.

'I really hope not,' she replied. 'I've got a **bad feeling** about that dude.'

I put the **Glove of Life** back in my pocket and we went looking for the others. We were thrilled to discover Billy Bob had set up an **ice-cream stall** on the basketball court. For only two dollars, Billy Bob was giving everyone a huge tub with **all ten flavours** in it!

We rushed over to join Kenny, Tiffany and the rest of our class in the queue.

Gary the Gorilla appeared and queued up behind me and Sarah.

When Sarah and I reached the front of the line, Sarah insisted on buying my ice-cream. 'It's the least I can do after you . . .'

'Shhhh!' I said, subtly pointing to Gary the Gorilla.

The ten-flavoured ice-cream tub was **Soooooo good**. Even the roast beef, fish and chips, and spaghetti scoops tasted amazing!

But ten scoops was **way too many!** We were so full that we lay on our backs like upturned turtles.

'I never want to eat ice-cream again,' I groaned.

'Nelson, can I borrow two dollars for another tub?' Kenny asked.

'How can you **still** be hungry?!' I exclaimed. 'I'm more full than a centipede's sock drawer!'

'The ice-cream is so yummy!' Kenny said.

'I'll see how much money I've got left,' I replied. But when I reached into my pocket, I had a horrible realisation. 'The Glove of Life . . . **it's gone!**'

'This is bad,' I said.

'Really bad,' Sarah added.

'Really, really bad,' Kenny said.

Sarah, Tiffany, Kenny and I searched the schoolyard for Grandma's glove. We looked all around Billy Bob's ice-cream stall. We looked behind the gym. And we searched **everywhere** in between.

'Gary the Gorilla was standing behind us in the ice-cream queue,' Sarah said. 'Do you think he could have . . . **stolen it?**'

'Why would Gary steal it?' Kenny said. 'Gorillas don't even wear gloves.'

'You do know that Gary's not a **real** gorilla?' Tiffany said.

We went looking for Gary, but he'd disappeared.

I was **So angry** with myself. Why didn't I keep it safe while I was waiting for the ice-cream?

'Grandma is going to be **MADDER** than I've ever seen her!' I said.

'You know what might make her feel better?' Kenny said. 'Ice-cream!'

SiX

On the way home from school, I was walking slower than a koala with a broken toe.

When we reached Main Street, Kenny stopped suddenly. He pointed to a television through a shop window . . .

'Is that **Gary the Gorilla?!**'

Kenny and I watched the news story unfold. Gary the Gorilla had zapped all the **baddie toys** in the Duck Creek Toy Shop with Grandma's glove and

brought them to life!

Then the baddie toys **DESTROYED** all the goody toys in the shop!

'Surely this **really, really bad** day can't get any worse?' I said.

'It **really, really can,**' Kenny replied. '**Look!**'

The baddie toys were now

chasing

everyone out of town!

There was a scary-looking **wizard** and huge **dragons** breathing fire.

There were cranky toy penguins sliding along the ground and toppling people over.

There were monkeys **clanging** cymbals and scaring people with the noise.

There were evil clowns shooting **lasers** out of their eyes!

And there were three-headed dog monsters scowling, **snarling** and scaring the pants off everyone. (Not actually, of course!)

'Are you thinking what I'm thinking?' I asked Kenny.

'Yeah,' Kenny replied. 'Time for **NINJA KID** and **H-DUDE** to make an appearance!'

We rushed behind the shops to change into our disguises.

When we returned to Main Street as Ninja Kid and H-Dude, the toys had chased even **more** people out of town.

We heard a helicopter above. The helicopter was familiar, but there was an unfamiliar face leaning out of it . . .

It was Gary the Gorilla. He was shouting through a megaphone.

'What's he saying?' Kenny asked.

'No idea!' I replied.

Gary's voice was so muffled, he was impossible to understand.

Then Gary removed the head of his gorilla costume . . . it was **DR KANE!**

'Whoa!' Kenny exclaimed. 'Did you know Gary the Gorilla was Dr Kane?'

'I had my suspicions,' I replied.

'Really?' Kenny said. 'I had absolutely **no idea.**'

As the helicopter drew closer, we realised it was being flown by **EINSTEIN**, Dr Kane's trusty chipmunk sidekick. The **ULTIMATE NINJA** sat in the back of the helicopter. I was sure that was my dad!

The townspeople were running and screaming as the evil toys chased them.

'That's it! Run, you cowards!' Dr Kane yelled through the megaphone.

Kenny and I started fighting off the baddie toys. We **flipped**, **kicked**, **twisted** and **tackled** as many as we could.

'Ninja Kid and H-Dude!' Dr Kane bellowed from the helicopter. 'We've been expecting you!'

'Don't you ever get **bored** of being pure evil?' I replied.

'Nope!' Dr Kane exclaimed gleefully.

'Being evil is **waaaaay too much fun!'** Einstein chipped in.

'I'm guessing you kids aren't good at maths!' Einstein shouted. 'So let me help you out. There are **two** of you and **heaps** of angry toys! You **can't win!**'

The chipmunk cackled. So did Dr Kane. The Ultimate Ninja just stared straight ahead.

The baddie toys kept coming at us. While Kenny was fighting off a **CLOWN**, a monkey crept up behind him and tried to **squash** Kenny between his cymbals. I did a spinning kick, sending the monkey and his cymbals flying!

While I was **leaping** over a ***sliding*** penguin, another clown aimed his laser eyes directly at me. Kenny quickly snatched a cymbal off a monkey and hurled it at the clown just in time.

As we fought off the evil toys, the townspeople continued streaming past us, including two very familiar faces . . .

'Need some help, Ninja Kid and H-Dude?' Sarah asked.

'Absolutely!' I exclaimed.

SEVEN

Sarah and Tiffany grabbed either end of a fallen branch and stopped a bunch of clowns in their tracks.

I used my ninja discs to repel the three-headed dog.

And Kenny used a **turbo-powered** hose to combat a fire-breathing dragon.

But Einstein the chipmunk was right, we were massively outnumbered.

'You will **NEVER** stop my toy army!' Dr Kane yelled at us.

He **laughed** into his megaphone. Then Einstein snatched the megaphone off Dr Kane and laughed into it, too.

'You're right!' I yelled back. 'We can't defeat you and your toys. You've **won** this time, Dr Kane.'

Kenny, Sarah and Tiffany looked at me in **TOTAL** disbelief. So did Einstein and the Ultimate Ninja.

'You don't know how **happy** it makes me to hear you admit **defeat!**' Dr Kane said.

'It doesn't make me happy,' Kenny said.

'Yeah, what are you talking about, Ninja Kid?' Sarah asked.

'Go with me on this, guys,' I whispered.

The others nodded, even though they had no idea what I was planning.

'Now that you've won, please **don't** turn us into toys!' I pleaded with Dr Kane.

Kenny looked at me quizzically then turned back to Dr Kane. 'Yeah, becoming a toy would be **terrible!**'

'My **worst** nightmare!' Tiffany added.

'What are you lot gibbering about?' Dr Kane asked. 'How on earth would I turn you into toys?'

'Oops,' I said, pretending.

'Hang on,' Dr Kane said. 'The **Glove of Life** could work in reverse and turn humans into toys!'

'Forget I said anything!' I replied.

'Ninja Kid's always saying completely ridiculous things,' Kenny added.

'Pass me the glove!' Dr Kane bellowed at Einstein.

'Dr Kane,' I pleaded. 'Before you turn us into toys forever, can we do one final thing as humans?'

'Urgh,' Dr Kane sighed. 'What is it?'

'Dance!' I exclaimed.

'Dance?' Kenny asked under his breath.

'Well, I suppose you'll never move again once you are toys,' Dr Kane said. 'So fine. Dance. But make it **quick!**'

'Three, two, one!' Sarah shouted.

We all started dancing! Sarah and Tiffany were **awesome** dancers. Me and Kenny . . . not so much. But we gave it our very best.

'This is awful!' Dr Kane said.

'I'm quite enjoying it,' Einstein said.

The Ultimate Ninja didn't seem to know what was going on.

I started adding **flips** into my dance moves, and while Dr Kane was watching Kenny attempt a **head spin**, I flipped extra high and **snatched** the Glove of Life off Dr Kane's hand!

Dr Kane turned to Einstein and the Ultimate Ninja. 'Why didn't you fools **stop** him?!'

'Don't blame us,' Einstein said. 'You were the one who said they could do a final dance!'

'You should have **done something!**' Dr Kane yelled at the Ultimate Ninja. The Ultimate Ninja just stared at him.

While Dr Kane and Einstein bickered, the four of us hid behind the shops.

'Awesome dance **distracting!'** I said.

'Nimble glove **snatching!'** Sarah replied.

'Can the glove really turn humans into toys?' Tiffany asked.

'Not that I know of!' I replied.

'So, are we going to turn the baddies back into toys?' Kenny asked.

'It would take too long,' I said. 'Plus, I can't risk Dr Kane getting the glove again.'

'That makes sense,' Sarah said. 'So what are we going to do?'

'We're going to **fight toys with toys!'** I announced.

'Brilliant idea!' Kenny said. 'But what on earth are you talking about?!'

'We need to gather as many goody toys as we can,' I explained, 'and use the Glove of Life **on them.'**

'We should start with the Toy Shop,' Tiffany said.

'We can't,' Kenny said. 'The baddie toys **destroyed** all the goody toys in the Toy Shop.'

'Then let's grab our own toys from home,' Sarah said.

'Great idea,' I replied. 'We'll meet back at the old water tower.'

We did a four-way fist bump to seal the deal.

EiGHT

In record time, Kenny, Sarah, Tiffany and I returned with all our toys. Between us, we had Wolf Girl and Sunrise, the Golden Unicorn, Minotaur, Skydragon, Griffin, E-boy, a muscly teddy bear, Kenny's sloth, Speedy, and heaps of other cool toys.

By now, Dr Kane's **evil** toy army had chased almost everyone out of Duck Creek.

'Soon there's going to be no-one left to save,' Sarah said.

'Everyone will come back once we've got rid of the baddie toys,' I replied.

'Let's do this!' Tiffany said.

I put on Grandma's **Glove of Life** and aimed it at our toys. I really, **really** needed it to work.

I was so nervous I closed my eyes as I pressed the button . . .

Our favourite toys **sprang** to life!

It was a **mind-blowing** sight!

We were still **outnumbered**, but now that we had the goody toys on our side, we had a fighting chance.

'Alright, gang!' I said. 'Let's **take down** some baddies!'

We formed a line in front of the evil toys.

'**Ha!**' Dr Kane scoffed from his helicopter. 'You really think that **ragtag** bunch can defeat my evil toy army?'

'I really do!' I replied.

'I really do, too!' Kenny added.

'Same!' Sarah said.

'Same! Same!' Tiffany said.

'You don't **all** need to respond to my questions!' Dr Kane replied. Then he turned to his toy army.

The evil toys took their **evilness** up a notch, but the goody toys were up for the challenge.

My E-boy toy had grown into a boy who was part robot, part human. He could control anything computerised, and he used this power to make all the remote-control clowns crash into one another!

Tiffany's Skydragon toy had the power to control insects, and she made a **SWARM OF BEES** attack the fire-breathing dragons! One little sting and the dragons crashed to the ground!

'**Get up**, you useless beasts!' Dr Kane yelled.

But the dragons rolled around on the ground, sore from the stings.

Kenny's Minotaur toy used its **incredible strength** to throw an abandoned fire truck at a bunch of life-sized toy **ROBOTS!**

Golden Unicorn grabbed the enormous hose from the fire truck and ran around and around a huge group of toys.

She was ***Sooooo fast*** that the toys were tied up by the hose before they even realised what Golden Unicorn was doing!

Wolf Girl climbed on top of Sunrise and they **charged** through a pack of penguins, **knocking** them to the ground like they were tenpin bowling pins.

Kenny's sloth, Speedy, was **So slow** that he wasn't much help battling the evil toys!

But he was very encouraging.

'Gooooo, Teeeeeaaaammmm!' he shouted in his very slow drawl.

We did our bit, too. I **jumped high** in the air and then executed a windmill kick which floored a row of angry robots.

Kenny darted around a dog monster so many times it got DIZZY and its three heads banged into one another.

Sarah teased the clowns, then dived out of the way just as they **fired** their laser eyes . . . and they took down a group of cymbal-crashing monkeys instead!

Tiffany lured all the **ANGRY** teddy bears to a **teddy bear picnic** then tied them up in a picnic blanket!

Eventually, all the evil toys were knocked down, tied up, or out of breath. I quickly used the **Glove of Life** on each of them, returning them all back to normal toys.

The glove worked **first time**, every time. Seemed it just needed a lot of warming up!

Turning the baddies back into toys was satisfying. But turning the goodies back into toys was **emotional**. In a very short time, we'd all grown quite fond of our lively life-size toys.

'I'm really sorry I have to do this,' I said.

'We understand,' Wolf Girl replied.

Sunrise howled in support.

'I'll **miss you** so much!' Sarah said.

'You'll still have us as toys,' Wolf Girl said.

Sarah nodded. Tiffany put her arm around her friend.

'One more hug!' Kenny said to Speedy.

'Of couuuuuuuuurse!' Speedy replied slowly.

I took a deep breath then aimed the glove at the goody toys . . .

Skydragon was flying through the air when I zapped her, and so not only did I zap Skydragon . . . I zapped Dr Kane as well!

And turned him into a **tiny DR KANE toy!** Turns out the glove really **could** turn humans into toys!

'What's happened to me?!' Dr Kane the talking toy cried out in a tiny voice.

Einstein cracked up laughing. So did the Ultimate Ninja!

'What are you fools giggling about?!' tiny Dr Kane screamed.

'You look so cute,' Einstein replied.

'Don't **ever** call me cute!' Dr Kane barked.

NOW!'

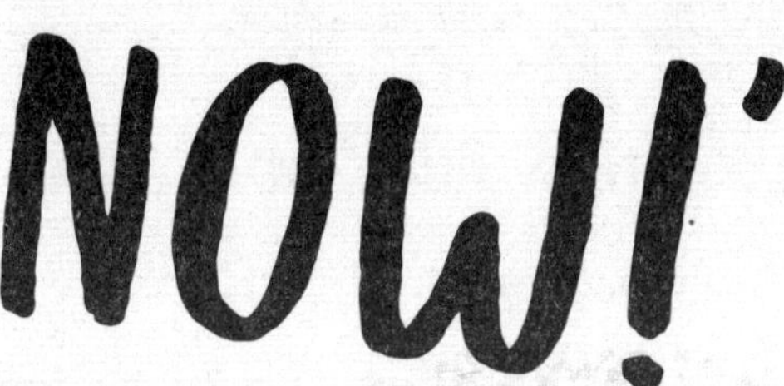

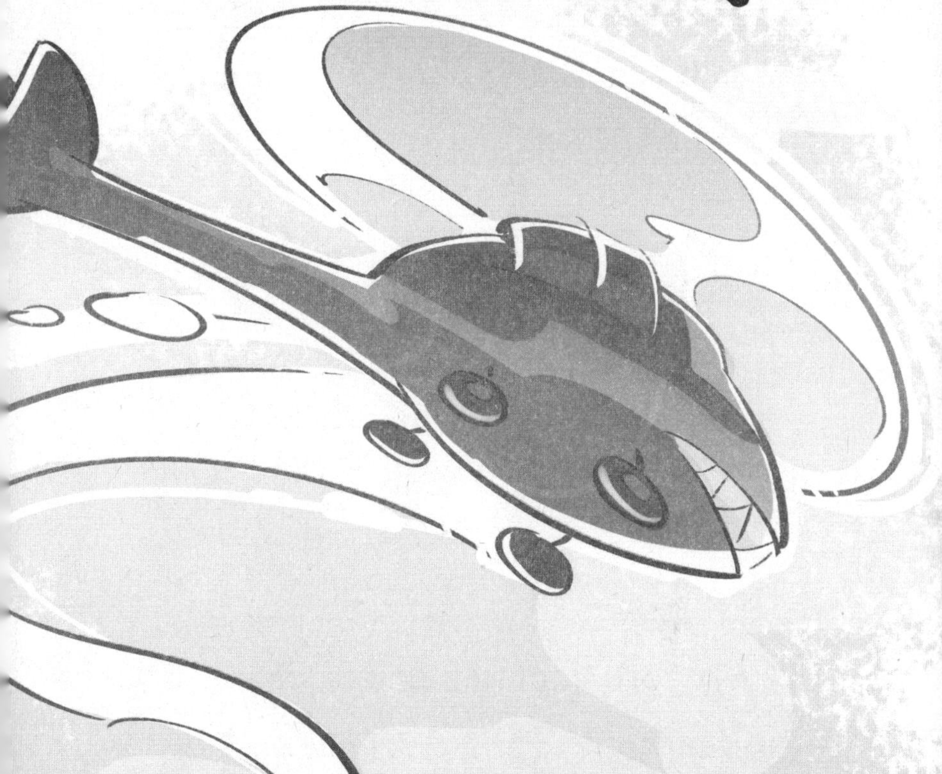

'Copy that, Boss,' Einstein said. 'You *little cutie!*'

As they flew away, the Ultimate Ninja stared at me. It felt like he was looking straight into my soul, as if he'd known me his whole life. Every part of me wanted to scream out, 'Dad!'

But before I could call out, they disappeared into the distance.

'You will pay for this, Ninja Kid!' Dr Kane screamed in his tiny voice.

'You will pay!'

As word spread that the evil toys had been defeated, the people of Duck Creek streamed back into town.

'You two were **amazing!'** Kenny said to Tiffany and Sarah.

'Yeah, you don't need superpowers to save the day!' I said.

'Maybe not,' Sarah said. 'But if there are any floating around, please let us know!'

When Billy Bob returned to town with his parents, he gave us all a huge thumbs up. 'Thanks for saving Duck Creek, you legends!'

Charles was not so grateful. 'You could have saved it quicker! We were already halfway out of town!'

'Has anyone seen Nelson and Kenny?' Sarah asked.

'Nope,' Tiffany replied. 'They always seem to **miss** all the action.'

H-Dude and I tried not to smile!

NiNE

When Kenny and I arrived home, we told Grandma and Mum all about our **MASSIVE** day.

Mum and Grandma were relieved we'd managed to drive Dr Kane out of Duck Creek. **Again!** But they were very disappointed we'd taken Grandma's **Glove of Life**.

'If you didn't take the glove,' Mum said, 'it wouldn't have ended up in the hands of Dr Kane.'

'And you wouldn't have needed to save the day,' Grandma said.

'Usually, when you don't want us to take something,' Kenny said. 'You tell us.'

'I thought you boys were old enough to know you can't just take something that belongs to someone else without asking.'

'We are old enough,' I said. 'We **panicked**. I'm so sorry, Grandma.'

'It was all my fault,' Kenny said. 'I drank Nelson's volcano soft drink and ate his lollies. Then I came up with the idea to use the **Glove of Life** for his Science Fair project.'

'It's my fault, too. I was the one that actually took the glove,' I said.

'We appreciate you both taking responsibility,' Mum said.

'And we're very proud of you for fighting off Dr Kane and his evil toys,' Grandma said.

'You're definitely on a **winner** with the Glove of Life,' Kenny said. 'It's life-changing. **Literally!**'

'What are you going to do with it?' I asked.

'Hide it in the shed,' Grandma said.

'Yeah,' Kenny laughed. '**Good one,** Grandma.'

'I'm serious,' Grandma replied. 'It's far **too powerful.**'

'Was your dad with Dr Kane again?' Mum asked.

I nodded. 'It's strange. He just stares blankly most of the time.'

'He's been **hypnotised** by Dr Kane,' Grandma reminded us. 'He's not really himself, but just a shell of himself waiting for Dr Kane's orders.'

'That must be incredibly hard on you,' Mum said, taking my hand.

'It's hard on all of us,' I replied.

'But everything will be so much better now Dr Kane is a tiny **toy** for the rest of his life!' Kenny said.

'I taught him everything I know about inventing,' Grandma said. 'He'll soon find a way to become his **fully-grown self** again.'

'His fully-grown **nasty** self,' Mum added.

'I wish we could break the spell Dr Kane has over Dad,' I said.

'Don't worry,' Grandma said. 'I'm working on it.'

'In the meantime,' Mum said, 'who's up for **ice-cream?**'

'Urgh!' I replied. 'I'm still **full**. I never want to eat ice-cream again!'

'I'll have Nelson's share!' Kenny said.

READ THEM ALL!

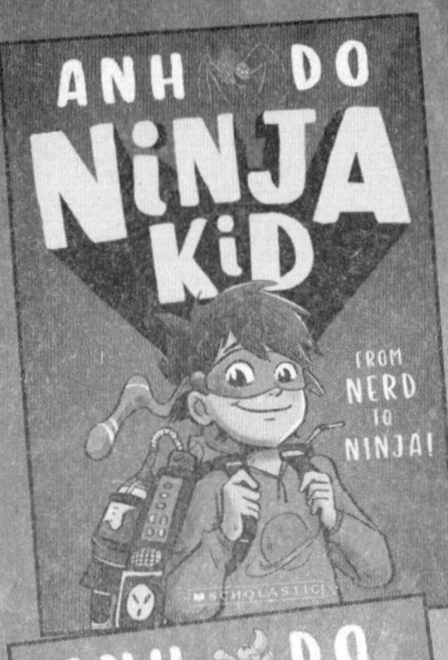

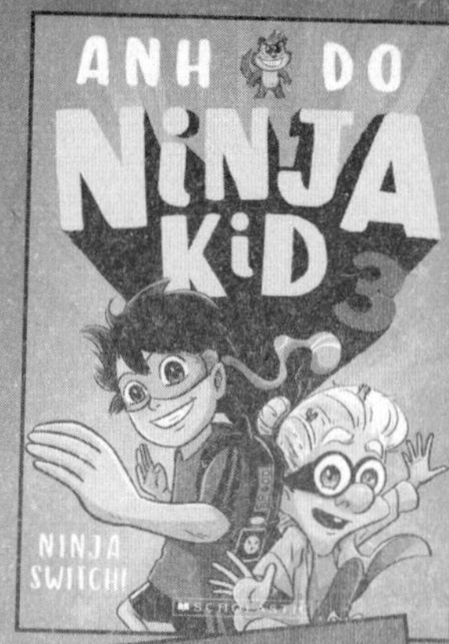

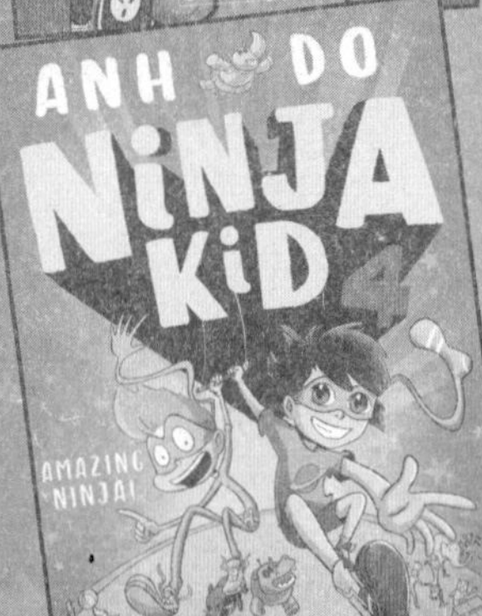

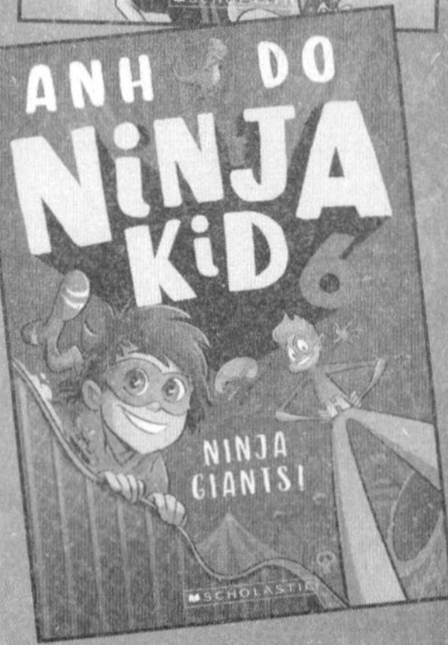

NINJA KID 8

COMING SOON!